Praise for *Faith Families for Le~ Easter, & Resurrec*~

"Traci Smith has done it a~ ~~ *,* *Easter, & Resurrection,* Sm~ ~tuition be our guide us as we journ~ ~gh Lent and then celebrate the season of ~e is as clear and engaging as ever, providing fre~ ~nd engaging prompts and practices that can be done in the 'holy mess' of family life. I highly recommend!"—**Jennifer Grant, author of** *Maybe God Is Like That Too* **and** *Dimming the Day*

"*Faithful Families: For Lent, Easter, & Resurrection* by Traci Smith is an excellent resource for anyone who has struggled to share the more difficult portions of the Jesus story with children during this high holiday season. From the reminder that we are the stuff stars are made of on Ash Wednesday, all the way throughout Lent, and culminating in Easter's focus on Resurrection, the triumph of life, hope, and justice shines bright for our little congregants. This is the book I wish had existed when my children were young. Whether you are a parent or involved in children's ministry desiring a better approach to sharing the gospel narratives during the Easter season, this book will help you do so in honest yet healthy, age-appropriate, and life-giving ways. I unreservedly and passionately recommend this timely and much needed volume."—**Herb Montgomery, Director, Renewed Heart Ministries**

"In her typical, easy-to-read, accessible style, Traci Smith offers yet another thoughtfully-penned, practical resource in her popular Faithful Families series that will be welcomed by progressive pastors and parents alike. If you buy only one book for the Easter season, make it this one." — **Glenys Nellist, author of *'Twas the Morning of Easter and Good News! It's Easter!***

"Family rituals for Lent and Easter without a disproportionate focus on blood? Yes, please! The gentle suggestions in this book of practices will be a perfect fit for gentle parents wanting to mark this particular season of the church calendar." — **Cindy Wang Brandt, Author of *You are Revolutionary* and *Parenting Forward***

"Traci Smith's book isn't just for faithful families—it's for holy households! People of all ages can choose from Traci Smith's collection of creative, reflective practices and prayers to deepen their journey with God in Lent, Easter, and the season of the Resurrection." — **Wendy Claire Barrie, Author of *Faith at Home: A Handbook for Cautiously Christian Families* and *The Church Post-Sunday School: How to Be Intergenerational and Why It Matters***

"Faithful Families is the resource families need as they move through Lent, Easter, and the Resurrection. Smith's theological and historical grounding draws readers into the purpose of preparation and celebration and inspires them to respond. In a time that is shadowed by overwhelm and anxiety, she offers a simple invitation alongside practical suggestions families can try as they journey through this holy season together. Families will be encouraged and strengthened in their love for God and each other." — **Rev. Dr. Tanya Marie Eustace Campen, Intergenerational Discipleship, Rio Texas Conference, United Methodist Church**

FAITHFUL FAMILIES

FOR LENT, EASTER, & RESURRECTION

SIMPLE WAYS TO CREATE
MEANING FOR THE SEASON

FAITHFUL FAMILIES

FOR LENT, EASTER, & RESURRECTION

A companion to *Faithful Families:
Creating Sacred Moments at Home*

TRACI SMITH

chalice
press

Saint Louis, Missouri

An imprint of Christian Board of Publication

Cover design and art: Paul Soupiset
Interior design: Connie H.C. Wang

ChalicePress.com

PRINT: 9780827211414
EPUB: 9780827211421
EPDF: 9780827211438

Printed in the United States of America

This one's for you, Mom. Every good idea I've ever had came from you. Thank you for teaching me how to treasure all the good things life has to offer.

Contents

Introduction

When I was a child, Easter meant new shiny white shoes, a bonnet, and a spring dress—usually covered up with a winter coat in our chilly Chicago climate. Easter meant jelly beans and chocolate bunnies, plastic eggs and fake grass. Easter meant church, too: a brass quartet, lilies, flowers on the cross.

As I got older, new layers of meaning unfolded around the Easter story. I began to gain awareness that there were dark, heavy, and sad parts to the narrative—namely, that Jesus was *tortured* and killed before he rose from the dead. Though these details were hard to absorb, I appreciated the cyclical nature of death and life. Something dies, and there is new life.

Over time, the theological meaning of Easter took on a new and richer meaning, as did the season of Lent preceding it. I started to understand the history and importance of a reflection period before Easter and began to appreciate the season of celebrating new life and resurrection as well.

In *Faithful Families for Lent, Easter, and Resurrection*, we'll go on a journey together and explore simple ways to experience all the richness this important season has to offer. If the season feels daunting or confusing, either on a personal level or in sharing with your family, you are not alone. I invite you to find where you connect to the story most strongly and choose the pieces of this story you'd like to highlight for yourself and for your family. There are far more ideas in this book than you could use in one year. Read through and focus on the ones that speak to you, and let your intuition be your guide.

What Is Lent?

Lent is the Christian season of holy preparation before Easter. It is the forty-six days from Ash Wednesday until Easter. Traditionally, Lent is a time for prayer, fasting, and giving. There are great variations in the ways Christians celebrate Lent, and many Christians emphasize their own traditions and values. This book presents a variety of different tools, rooted in mainline Protestant practice and theology. I hope you feel free to use the ideas here as a canvas on which to paint your own traditions, old and new.

What Is Holy Week?

The final week of Lent is called Holy Week. Holy Week is considered the most significant week in the Christian calendar, and includes Palm Sunday, Maundy Thursday, Good Friday, and Holy Saturday.

What Is Easter?

Easter is the day Christians celebrate the resurrection of Jesus Christ from the dead. This day, which we now call Easter, was the beginning of the movement we now call Christianity. It is the most important day of the Christian year. We celebrate Easter not on a specific date, but on a day referred to as a "moveable feast." Specifically, Easter happens on the first Sunday on or following the spring equinox. (If that's confusing for you, do as I do and ask Google to tell you the date!)

Though Easter has very specific (and important!) religious significance for Christians, it is celebrated broadly in our culture. Symbols of Easter can be both religious and non-religious. Many parents trying to teach their children the spiritual and religious significance of Easter want to keep the holiday free of secular (non-religious) symbols such as the Easter Bunny, jelly beans, or Easter eggs. In my view, these secular symbols can add to the celebration of the holiday and even enrich our celebration of it. For this reason, you will find a variety of both religious and non-religious symbols in the pages of this book. I stop short of including the bunny—although the Easter Bunny certainly makes an appearance at our house, and the basket is proudly displayed right alongside our other Easter symbols!

What Is the Season of Resurrection?

Christians often speak of resurrection as a singular event— the day Jesus rose from the dead. And yet our church calendar lists Easter not as a single day, but as a season. In *Faithful Families for Lent, Easter, and Resurrection,* I acknowledge this with a full chapter dedicated to resurrection practices. As you try out these ideas, you may begin to see resurrection not only as a singular event, but a full season of celebration.

Theological Notes for the Season

Theology is the study of God. Just like other "ologies" (geology, ornithology, and psychology, to name a few), there are experts—with or without PhDs—and hundreds of thousands of pages written about the various nuances of theology. When we talk to children about faith or practice faith at home, we are *doing* theology (whether we realize it or not). We are living into the study of God. The faith practices in this book are deeply informed by my own theological perspective, though I leave plenty of room for your family and church community to decide how best to interpret them and incorporate them into your family's life.

Because the seasons of Lent and Easter deal with the *heart* of the Christian faith, I've felt it necessary to add a few theological notes to help you guide your family through the season. If something I say here inspires your family to dive even deeper into theological study, I wish you well on that journey and invite you to consult the "For Further Reading" list found at www.traci-smith. com. If you'd rather not engage in further study, there is no requirement for you to do so. I've done the work of vetting these practices for you, leaving them in what I consider a theological safe zone, neither committing you to fundamentalist or damaging theologies nor making specific statements likely to fall outside the realm of your congregation's orthodoxy. These practices are, in many ways, a blank canvas on which you can paint the images most suited to your own tradition and norms. My great hope is that this book is both flexible enough for you to interpret and structured enough for you to find direction and purpose.

Trauma and the Violence of the Cross

Though I bristle at the word "expert," I've spent a great portion of my career studying faith formation. In addition to researching and writing books about faith practices at home, I regularly speak to groups of Christian educators, ministry professionals, and parents. Over the years I've heard countless stories about the lasting damage that can be done when violent stories of the Bible are told in ways that are inappropriate for a child's age and emotional development.

The bloody and violent details of the crucifixion story are difficult to process, even for adults. Though I advocate tackling difficult topics with children, I do not advocate exposing them unnecessarily to the violent details of the torture, crucifixion, and death of Jesus Christ. The *Faithful Families* perspective is that violent imagery and symbols should be discussed and incorporated into the story with extreme caution, not because they are unimportant or to be glossed over, but because they are an unnecessary burden for children to carry. An undue focus on violent imagery distracts from the message of the gospel, putting the emphasis not on resurrection and new life where it belongs, but stuck, like a skipped record, on death, torture, and violence.

This book does not look the other way when it comes to difficult subjects such as death, suffering, and grief. In fact, you will find many prayers, practices, and conversation starters to help you and your family navigate the waters of these tough topics. That being said, those practices, prayers, and conversation starters deliberately avoid centering the symbols and stories related to the torture and violent death of Jesus because they are not appropriate for all ages.

What is the right age for parents and Christian educators to bring up these harder details of the story? This is a hard question to answer, and it depends greatly on the individual child. As a general rule of thumb, I believe middle school-age is the earliest we should start to discuss the violent and traumatic details of the story.

Atonement Theory and the Meaning of Jesus' Death

The phrase "Jesus died for our sins" is so common in Christian churches (and even in popular culture) that we rarely give it much thought. What does it mean to say, "Jesus died for our sins?" What is the relationship between *sin* and *death*? The Easter story is about death and resurrection. What is the meaning of Jesus' death, specifically, and human death, generally? What is sin? These questions might appear, at first glance, to have simple answers. When we speak to children, we try to make the answers even simpler for them to digest. Yet a statement like "Jesus died for you" or "Jesus died for our sins," while simple, carries tremendous weight and conveys complicated theological meaning.

In Christian theology, "atonement" is the reconciliation of God and humanity through Jesus Christ. During two thousand years of Christian history, the church has explained atonement in a variety of different ways, using a variety of different metaphors and scriptures. Some of these theories, on the surface, sound like simple and orthodox Christian theologies; but when we peel back what's really being said, we find a theological message that can be quite damaging for children. Is God an angry God who demands innocent blood? Did God *trade* Jesus' life for *ours*? Is the torture and death of Jesus a good and meaningful necessity in order to satisfy God's need for justice? For me, the answer to all these questions is a resounding *no;* I would never describe the mission, purpose, and death of Jesus in this way. It is possible to understand Jesus' life and mission on earth without using the explanations above, all of which are atonement theories.

This book is my attempt to give you hands-on practices, stories, prayers, and ideas that teach about the life, death, and resurrection of Jesus Christ in a way that both acknowledges the hard and sad details of the story while keeping the focus on the resurrecting work of Christ.

Answering the question "What does the death of Jesus mean?" is a lifelong pursuit. There is room for a variety of faithful perspectives. It is my hope that this book will provide space for you and your family to explore these difficult topics in an honest and open way, acknowledging the hard realities of death without imposing a rigid or simplistic theological framework. For those who wish to explore atonement theology further, please visit www. traci-smith.com

Honoring and Embracing Mystery

Those who are familiar with my first book, *Faithful Families: Creating Sacred Moments at Home,* know that I am a strong proponent of using the word *mystery* with children. Mystery invites us into something deep within ourselves, the universe, and the world around us, and acknowledges that we do not know everything. "It's a mystery" is a great way to acknowledge some of the most profound aspects of our Christian faith. How did Jesus rise from the dead? What does resurrection mean? These are deep and important mysteries. Mystery says, "I don't know" without saying "I don't care." Just as there are many perspectives on death, there are many perspectives on resurrection. What is my own view? Well, quite simply, I believe resurrection is a profound mystery.

Blessings to you and your family as you embark on this journey through the mysteries of faith.

NOTES FOR PARENTS

On Letting Things Go and Trade-offs

Our time is finite. When we choose to do something, we are, by definition, choosing *not* to do other things. A decision to spend time with family is a decision to not spend that time working, cleaning, shopping, or attending holiday gatherings. As much as we'd like to think we can "do it all," we can't. The practices in this book invite you to consciously choose time with your family *instead of* some other things. If you approach this book as another to-do list on top of an already full and busy life, you will make yourself crazy! Instead, choose to say no to some other things the season offers.

Finding Rest as a Parent

As a minister, my colleagues often remind me that I can't pour out for others that which I don't have myself. One cannot drink from an empty well. The same is true for parents and children. If you'd like to create sacred and holy moments for your family, you must first start from a place of peace and balance within yourself. It is not selfish, as a parent, to take time for rest and renewal before creating something special for your children and family. If you're exhausted, rest. If you need to seek counsel or healing, do that before trying to create a perfect space for others. If this is not the year to do the practices in this book, set it aside. It will be here next year. Take care of yourself, first and foremost, so that you may have an abundance to share with your family.

Being Gentle When Things Don't Go Perfectly

One constant in family life: Things rarely go as planned. I've embarked on many a family activity, project, or faith moment with my children only to have things end up straying quite far from the original plan. Sometimes children don't want to participate; they get the wiggles or act out. Sometimes I find I'm much grumpier than I thought I was, and act impatiently. Sometimes we must just let the moment go. But then, there are times when a sacred moment just appears, seemingly out of nowhere. I cherish those moments! It is wise to approach the practices in this book with a sense of lightness. Don't hold too tightly to them. Expect that some will fall flat, while others may surprise you with joy. It's unrealistic to think that every family moment will be a smashing success. Families are messy, and sometimes there is beauty in that holy mess. Try to laugh it off when things don't go as planned. ("Well, *that* was something!") We can try again tomorrow.

A Word on Repetition

The beauty in these practices comes through the repetition. Plowing through every practice in this book is probably not as effective as picking a few practices and repeating them weekly or (in the case of some prayers) daily. Picking a practice or two and repeating them annually over many years is also a powerful way to create lasting memories. Choose quality over quantity, repetition over novelty.

A NOTE ON AGES

Finding activities that are meaningful for family members of all ages can be a challenge. The practices in this book are designed for families with children of all ages. Here are some specific tips for children at the younger and older ends of the spectrum.

Tips for Younger Children

- Remember attention spans. For the littlest ones, two or three minutes is plenty of time.

- Adjust your expectations. If you don't get through the whole practice or prayer, that's okay. Do what you can, and remember that the goal is to spend time together.

- Ask young children to repeat the words of prayers after an adult says them, one line at a time.

- Where the practices call for writing something down, have young children draw pictures instead.

- Ask open-ended questions. Statements beginning with "I wonder..." also invite young children into the stories. For example: "I wonder what it was like to wave palm branches on the day Jesus rode a donkey into the city."

Tips for Older Children and Teens

- Offer choices. Give the book to them and let your children choose a practice or prayer.

- Ask them to lead. Children and teens may choose to do a practice in a different way with their own spin on it. Older children might prefer helping younger ones in the family with activities that feel too elementary for them.

- Invite feedback with open-ended questions. For example: "What do you think about this story?"

- Invite participation rather than requiring it.

NOTES FOR MINISTRY LEADERS

I have the utmost respect for ministry leaders who are called to lead family ministries with children. One of the challenging parts of the job is balancing the needs of all people with whom you work: parents, children, families, volunteers, and coworkers. This resource is for families, but my hope is that ministry leaders will use it as well, modeling how these resources can benefit the families in your care. Here are some ways you can do that.

Give Parents a Place to Rest and Freedom from Perfection

I don't know many parents who never question whether or not they're doing it right. In fact, most parents I know find themselves constantly questioning their parenting abilities. When it comes to nurturing children toward a healthy spirituality, the questions become even more daunting. Some parents wonder if they have enough knowledge to teach their children, preferring to leave that teaching to church educators and pastors. As a ministry leader, it's up to you to encourage the parents in your care and remind them that perfection is not the aim. God is pleased with our wholehearted attempts to share with our children the gifts we have been given. Perfection is not the goal. Help your parents laugh when things go amusingly astray and celebrate the smallest of successes.

Model That Less Is More

If you gift this book to the families in your congregation, be sure to emphasize that there's an entire buffet of options here, and they needn't choose more than a few. You can act as curator and choose the practices you think work well with your congregation and ministry. You may want to choose a practice or two per week and highlight them for your congregation.

Teach These Practices as a Group, Then Practice at Home

As a parent, there's something comforting and helpful in knowing that we're not alone as we try new things with our families. Use your influence as a ministry leader to teach families these practices and keep them accountable (in a fun way) to do them. Have a "prayer of the week" that you teach during your time together, then ask families to pray it together during the week. Do the same with the practices. You could even empower families to do the activities by getting materials ready and directing them to the appropriate page or practice.

Find Rest as a Ministry Leader

Whenever I write for families, I have ministry leaders in mind as well. How can you use the practices in this book to make life easier for yourself? Perhaps one of the practices works well as a children's message or a devotional. Maybe it kickstarts your imagination and leads you to an activity you'd like to do with your families in a workshop or teaching moment. Rest is important for you, too.

Permissions

By purchasing this book, your congregation is permitted to excerpt up to five prayers, practices, and lessons from this book in your church communications (newsletter, bulletin, etc.). When you do, please use the following attribution: "Excerpted from *Faithful Families for Lent, Easter, and Resurrection* by Traci Smith (Chalice Press: 2021, All Rights Reserved)."

Before the Season Begins: Set an Intention

I think of this book as a travel guide or cookbook. Rather than choosing each activity in order and working through them, pick and choose what works for you. Though there are dozens of practices, prayers, and ideas in this book, you're not expected to go through them all. I encourage you to quickly read through the book once, marking or noting the practices that appeal to you. Then, take a look at the ones you've marked. Is this a manageable number, or too many? Cull the list. I suggest no more than five to ten total practices or prayers for the season. You can write down your experience afterward and repeat the ones that worked well for you.

Before moving on to the rest of the book, it might be useful to take a moment and set an intention for what practices you are looking for. What kind of Lent, Easter, and Resurrection season are you trying to create for your family or congregation? Do you want to focus on prayer? service? fasting? Do you want this year to be simple and carefree, or do you have a bit of extra time to devote to something more in-depth or complicated? Do you need to be on the lookout for practices and prayers that work well for little ones, or are you celebrating with people who are a bit older?

Before continuing into the book, or after you've skimmed through it once, take a moment and write down a sentence or two about your intention for the season. You can set an intention individually or as a family. Do this by completing one or more of these sentences:

- This year we (I) would like Lent, Easter, and Resurrection to be...

- I hope that at the end of this Lent, Easter, and Resurrection season we (I)...

- Maybe during this Lent, Easter, and Resurrection season we (I)...

- One question we'd (I'd) like to answer during this Lent, Easter, and Resurrection season is...

If you know where you want to go, you will have a better chance of getting there. Not every recipe you try from a cookbook becomes a family favorite; not every destination from the travel guide becomes the best part of the trip. Likewise, there will be some surprises (and maybe some disappointments) in these pages. Keep an attitude of openness and experimentation, and keep moving forward, trying things as you go. May it be a holy time for your family and congregation.

Before the Season Begins: Create a Sacred Space

Think of a place that is sacred or holy to you. What makes it sacred? Perhaps you're imagining a place in nature where you feel connected to the creative power of the Holy Spirit.

Maybe there is a home you grew up in or visited where you felt loved or valued. Some people connect to a sacred place of worship, such as a sanctuary or cathedral.

Taking time to create a sacred space at home can serve as a focal point for your Lenten and Easter practice. Let this book live there, along with anything else you're using from the book. Create the sacred space as a gift to the other members of your household, or create it together. Here are three simple ways to create a sacred space, depending on the amount of time, space, and energy you can devote to it. I encourage you to use materials you have on hand rather than purchasing new ones. Here are some different ways to organize your sacred space.

- **Table Space:** Clear off a side table, nightstand, or buffet, or put up a small table. Cover the table with a purple cloth at the beginning of Lent, then change it to white on Easter morning. Rotate symbols of Lent, Easter, and Resurrection on the table. (Use chapters 3 and 9 for symbol ideas.) Place your prayer requests or candles on the table along with other sacred materials you used during Lent, Easter, and Resurrection.

- **Closet Space:** Clear out a closet or corner of a room. Hang up Christmas lights or place a lamp on a table. Add cushions, a comfy chair, or blankets to sit on. This sort of sacred space is meant to be a space to go to for quiet prayer or meditation, so put activities in the space for this purpose. Some ideas include a finger labyrinth, prayer book or beads, and headphones.

- **Shoebox Space:** For those without much space to set aside, find a small box—such as a shoebox or lunchbox—

and put a few sacred items inside. For example, start with a votive candle and a small notebook and pen. As the season unfolds, add to your box. Take it out when you're ready to spend holy time together as a family, or take turns spending time with it individually.

A Prayer for a Sacred Space

Thank you, God, for this space to use as we travel through the seasons of Lent, Easter, and Resurrection. May it be special to us. May we return to it often and say thank you for being in this space with us, as you always are everywhere with us.

Before the Season Begins: Make a Family Journal for the Season

When I was in college, there was a small prayer chapel in the lower level of my dorm. It was a simple space with a pew and small table set aside for private prayer. On the pew was a journal where people could write their prayers or thoughts. The collaborative nature of the book made it truly special. It didn't belong to just one person. Instead, each person added to it. Over time, it became a true treasure, and part of my prayer time became flipping through the prayer journal to see what others had offered to God in their prayers.

To make a journal for the season of Lent, Easter, and Resurrection, start with a simple notebook or journal. Each member of the family can add to the cover by pasting images from magazines (or their own created art) as a collage. Throughout the season of Lent, Easter, and Resurrection, take turns creating pages inside. The pages might contain written prayers, doodles, notes from any of the projects found in this book, photos, or other memories from the season.

Let the journal unfold with the season. Try not to put too many rules or parameters on what it must be or what it will become. For inspiration, do an internet search on "art journal" or "smash book."

You might divide the journal into three sections at the beginning: one for Lent, one for Holy Week and Easter, and one for Resurrection. Or you might let it unfold with the season.

It's fun to flip through the journal and take note of what you've learned and created.

Chapter 1: Beginning the Season

This chapter contains a handful of practices that are meant to orient your entire Lenten practice. They are designed to be practiced slowly and deliberately, a little each day. I recommend picking only one of the practices in this chapter to guide you through the whole season so you can give it your full focus and attention. You might experiment with a different practice each year and rotate through them, or you might find one you like and keep it year to year.

Count the Days with a Lenten Paper Chain

Using a paper chain to count the days is a fun and easy way to mark time. Though Christians typically think of Lent as 40 days long, those 40 days do not include Sundays. Adding in the Sundays (but not including Easter Sunday), Lent is 46 days long beginning with Ash Wednesday. To use a paper chain counting down Lent, either make 40 links and don't remove a link on Sundays, or make 46 links and remove one each day. The advantage of using a 46-link chain is that you are consistent with your daily practice. The advantage of a 40-link chain is that it mirrors the 40 days Jesus was in the wilderness. You can make your chain out of purple paper, the traditional color of Lent.

Alternatively, instead of using your paper chain to count down to Easter by removing a link each day, do the reverse and create a paper chain that grows each day from Ash Wednesday to Easter. If you do a paper chain that grows, you could consider writing a memory from the day on each link and watch your memories grow.

A Journey of Transformation: Witnessing Growth

One way to think of the spiritual process of Lent is as a journey. Sometimes the journey is as important (or more so) than the destination. Our Lenten journey is often one of personal transformation. Perhaps we're working toward becoming more grateful or more kind. Perhaps we want to pray more. Whatever our spiritual goals are, they are a process.

Help make this connection more concrete by growing something during Lent. When we grow something, we can see the concept of journey or transformation more clearly. Start your growing project by saying, "The Lenten season can be a time where we grow and change. All living things grow and change. Let's look at how these seeds (or plants) grow over time." You could choose to be informal about it, or you could keep a detailed diary in which you observe and write down the progress each day.

Here are some growing experiments that work well during Lent:

- Grow a bean sprout from a dried bean. This can be done in a wet paper towel or in a paper cup. Do an internet search for specific directions.

- Grow wheatgrass. Many ministry leaders have told me how easy this is, as wheatgrass survives a bit of inattention and grows well during this time of year. Wheatgrass is also called "cat grass" and is available for purchase in all-in-one kits with directions included.

- Grow mustard seeds in pots or in the garden. Follow the directions on the back of the seed packet.
- Grow amaryllis bulbs. Amaryllis bulbs grow and flower in about the same amount of time as the Lenten season. Part of the trick, though, is finding a bulb to plant. I have had good luck getting these during post-Christmas clearance sales and saving them until Lent.

Though it's nice to set yourself up for success by researching the seeds you'll use and caring for them to the best of your ability, consider the spiritual lesson if your seeds *don't* grow as well as you hoped (or at all). There are lessons to be learned in both the successes and the failures, so be open to whatever the experience brings you.

A Journey of Transformation: Smoothing Rough Edges

Rock tumbling is another great metaphor for transformation and growth. The rocks start out very rough and dull; slowly, through time and with lots of water and grit, they become smooth and shiny. If you're new to rock tumbling, do a quick internet search to learn the basics.

Rock tumbling can be done at home or in a larger group at church or school. You'll need a rock tumbler and the associated grits, along with the rocks. Each kit has its own directions and timeline, but many take about six weeks, the same time period as Lent. Invest in a rock tumbler and do this exercise every year during Lent, or try it once and pass your tumbler on to another family. Watch the rocks change and transform, and think about how your own life goes through a similar process.

Lenten Word-a-Day

A Lenten word-a-day calendar can add focus to your Lenten practice, as each day will have one word to explore. Lenten word-a-day calendars have become popular in recent years. This version is my adaptation of this practice. Take whatever calendar you already use (wall hanging, planner, or digital) and write one of the words below into each day's square. Put the first word on Ash Wednesday and the last word on Easter Sunday and fill the rest in between. Or you can simply write the words down on a piece of paper and cross one off each day. If you miss a day, pick up where you left off.

There are many ways to use your word-a-day each day of Lent:

- Draw a picture (or take a picture) of something that the word brings to mind.
- Write a journal entry using the word as a prompt.
- Use the word as a conversation starter for your household.
- Find a way to "do" the word: drink a cool glass of water for "water," or roll around in the yard for "tumble."
- Any combination of the above!

Day 1: Dust	Day 17: Earth	Day 33: Wonder
Day 2: Grow	Day 18: Towel	Day 34: Jesus
Day 3: Tumble	Day 19: Sunshine	Day 35: Travel
Day 4: Friend	Day 20: Rest	Day 36: Listen
Day 5: Peace	Day 21: Neighbor	Day 37: Still
Day 6: Soil	Day 22: Candle	Day 38: Root
Day 7: Water	Day 23: Thrive	Day 39: Quiet
Day 8: Air	Day 24: Rain	Day 40: Spirit
Day 9: Transform	Day 25: Wait	Day 41: Beauty
Day 10: Pray	Day 26: Human	Day 42: Tree
Day 11: Rock	Day 27: Cloud	Day 43: Thankful
Day 12: Rainbow	Day 28: Family	Day 44: Angel
Day 13: Create	Day 29: Free	Day 45: Shadow
Day 14: Release	Day 30: Light	Day 46: Silence
Day 15: Fly	Day 31: Journey	Day 47: Resurrection
Day 16: Butterfly	Day 32: Flower	

A Prayer for the Beginning of a Journey

As we begin the season of Lent, we look forward to going on a spiritual journey. May the time we spend in prayer, service, and reflection bring us closer to God and closer to one another. May we stay focused on our Lenten practice and have patience when we make mistakes or lose our way. Amen.

A Prayer for Focus During Lent

There are so many ways to spend our time this Lent.

Some feel energizing.

Some feel distracting.

Some are exciting.

Some are boring.

Help us to still our minds and bodies so that when we choose how to spend our precious time, we choose the things that make life brighter. Amen

A Prayer for Patience

We wait with patience to learn what new things God might teach us in this season. Sometimes patience means waiting. Sometimes patience means listening. Sometimes patience means asking questions. God, please help us understand what patience means this season. Amen.

As We Look for God's Presence

God, as we begin the season of Lent, Easter, and Resurrection, help us look for your presence...

in prayer,

in our spiritual practice,

in nature,

in one another.

Bless our days, that we may grow in faith, hope, and love. Amen.

Chapter 2: Pancake Tuesday and Ash Wednesday

Pancake Tuesday

Also known as Shrove Tuesday or Fat Tuesday (Mardi Gras), Pancake Tuesday is the day before Lent begins. The tradition began around A.D. 600 when Christians would give up all meat and animal products during Lent, so they used up their eggs, butter, and milk by making pancakes the day before. Christians have carried the tradition forward by having Pancake Tuesdays.

The word "shrove" in "Shrove Tuesday" refers to the absolution of sins and repentance. I tend toward leaving repentance out of the discussion on this day, trusting that the next day, Ash Wednesday, will provide plenty of opportunity to talk about the more somber aspects of the season.

I also avoid talking about gorging or overindulgence on Pancake Tuesday. As we'll discuss much more in chapter five, it is important to frame fasting and restrictions in a healthy way for children, and the idea that Pancake Tuesday is for stuffing ourselves to the point of discomfort is not a tradition I condone.

In other words: Let pancakes be pancakes, and don't overthink it! Pancake Tuesday can be as simple as that. Eat pancakes for dinner on the Tuesday before Ash Wednesday. This simple tradition helps to mark the season of Lent in a warm and simple way. Cook up your favorite pancake recipe and enjoy.

Understanding Ash Wednesday and Celebrating at Home

Ash Wednesday is the first day of the season of Lent. It is the Wednesday exactly 46 days before Easter Sunday. Ash Wednesday gets its name from a ritual in which a priest or pastor dips their finger in ashes and draws them on the foreheads of congregation members saying, "Repent and believe the good news of the gospel" or "Remember that you are dust, and to dust you shall return." The ashes are traditionally made by burning the palm branches from the previous year's Palm Sunday. This ritual marks the beginning of Lent and is a powerful reminder that life is fleeting, that each day is precious and valuable. The ashes are also a symbol of repentance, or turning away from sin.

In this chapter, we'll explore several practices and prayers for Ash Wednesday at home. It can feel heavy and somber to remind children of their eventual deaths (which is, after all, the heart of what Ash Wednesday teaches). One

Ash Wednesday many years ago, I was offering ashes to a group outside my regular worshipping congregation. Adults came forward and lifted up their hair as I said the words "Remember that you are dust, and to dust you shall return." One young mother, after receiving her ashes, bent down and picked up her baby from the stroller. She held the baby up to me and said, "Ashes for my daughter, too, please." I had rarely placed ashes on a baby before, so this moment struck me in a new way. Tears came to my eyes as I smudged ashes on the baby's tiny forehead and said, "Remember that you are dust, and to dust you shall return."

In thinking about that moment, and in considering how to handle Ash Wednesday with young children, I've come to embrace the value of this somber day even for the youngest among us. When we speak about the fragility of life and our eventual death in plain terms, with frank language, we do our children a great service. Rather than treating death as taboo or off-limits, we open the door to conversation and a rich spiritual practice wherein death, though certainly tragic and sad most of the time, is a normal and expected part of life.

We Come from Dust

In the book of Genesis, the very first book of the Bible, we read, "Then the Lord God formed man from the dust of the ground, and breathed into his nostrils the breath of life; and the man became a living being" (Genesis 2:7). In Hebrew, the original language of the book of Genesis, there is a very close link between the word ʿādām, meaning "man" or "human being," and ădāmâ, "ground." The *adam* was made from the *adama*: the human from the ground.

The image of God breathing into the dirt and creating humanity is a powerful one. What makes us different from a ceramic jar is God's breath in us, that close and intimate link between us and God. At the end of our lives, as our breath or spirit returns to God, our bodies will turn to dust again, either through cremation or decomposition into earth. On Ash Wednesday, you can remember this link at home by replacing ashes with dirt.

Take a small scoop of dirt from the ground and place it in a dish. Let each person in your family squish it around with their fingers. Read Genesis 2:7 and explain the connection between the word "ground" and the word "human." Explain, in simple language, that all people return to the earth after they die. Then, if you like, make a cross shape on the back of your hand and say, "Remember that you are dust, and to dust you shall return. Amen."

We Are the Stuff of Stars

When we think about our genesis, the world's beginning, we are not limited to the Bible's explanation. We can also think about what science teaches us about our origins. Though the church and the scientific community have found themselves at odds with each other over the centuries, this need not be the case. The Bible was never intended to be a scientific textbook. Instead, it offers a theological explanation for where we come from. Therefore, we are free to allow science to enrich and support our faith. When we approach both science and faith with a sense of wonder and mystery, it deepens our respect for both.

Science teaches us the "big bang theory," where particles exploded into the universe to create life. The very same matter that scattered throughout the universe so many billions of years ago became the building blocks for our bodies. We are, quite literally, the stuff of stars.

Today, on Ash Wednesday, we can remember our beginning and consider our place in this vast and ancient universe. One approach is researching the origins of the universe. Search the web for lectures or reflections that explain the newest theories about how the universe came to be. Study a new perspective. Take time to look at a map of the universe and consider just how many galaxies there are in addition to our own Milky Way. As you learn and explore, wonder aloud what your place is in this enormous universe. It is so big, and we are so small. Wonder aloud with those in your family. *I wonder how the universe got its start...*

The Symbolism of Ashes: *Memento Mori*

Memento mori is Latin for "Remember that you [have to] die." It's a weighty phrase, particularly for young children. And yet, philosophers, theologians, and artists have urged us to find ways to consider our eventual deaths as a reminder to appreciate life and never take it for granted. Furthermore, regularly remembering and honoring the truth that all living things die helps us to weather the inevitable grief we face when our loved ones *do* die.

The imposition of ashes and the phrase "Remember that you are dust, and to dust you shall return" is a *memento mori*. If you attend church on Ash Wednesday and receive the imposition of ashes, take some time to talk about what this symbol means to you. How does it feel to acknowledge that everyone will eventually die, including yourself? If the conversation becomes scary or hard for young ones in your home, take the opportunity to reassure children that when the time comes for them to grieve someone who dies, you will be present with them, helping them through.

If you will not receive the imposition of ashes, consider reflecting on a piece of art with a *memento mori* theme. To do this, conduct an image search on the phrase "vanitas art." I recommend an adult do this search to find an image that will provoke conversation but not be too frightening or severe for your children. The piece I like is called "Still Life with a Tulip, Skull, and Hourglass" by Philippe de

Champaigne,[1] As the name suggests, the piece has three symbols, each representing something different. The tulip represents life, the skull represents death, and the hourglass represents time. How do you feel when you look at this piece of art? What do you think it means? Close your discussion by sharing about the things in life that bring you joy.

---

[1] Philippe de Champaigne, *Vanitas Still Life with a Tulip, Skull and Hour-Glass,* c. 1671, oil on panel, Tessé Museum, Le Mans, France.

The Symbolism of Ashes: Turning Around

If you attend a church service on Ash Wednesday, one thing the pastor or priest might say while putting ashes on your forehead is, "Repent, and believe in the gospel." Simple and useful definitions of *repent* and *gospel* are "turn around" and "good news." So, simply stated, the ashes remind us to "Turn around and remember the good news." Why should we turn around? What are we turning away from? What are we turning toward? And what is the good news?

Before or after you receive ashes, consider making a list with two columns. In one column write, "Things I'd like to turn away from." In the other column write, "Things I'd like to turn toward." Look at each of these two lists and ponder the direction you would like your life to take. This activity can be individual or communal, shared out loud or quiet.

A Prayer for Ash Wednesday

On this day of ashes, we remember where we came from. The Bible tells us we came from the dust of the ground. Science tells us we came from the stuff of stars. May we believe in the mystery of both. We came from dust and from stardust. We are both. At the end of our lives, all living things return to the earth—including us. Our spirits belong to God, now and forever. Amen.

A Prayer about Ashes and Life

God, you are the source of all life and energy. We come from God, and we return to God. Life to life. Ashes to ashes. Energy to energy. Dust to dust. Amen.

A Prayer for Marking the Season

God, on this Ash Wednesday, this first day of Lent, we mark the beginning of our journey to Easter. We ask you to be with us as we learn about you in these 46 days. May this be a holy time in our family and in our lives. Amen.

Chapter 3: Praying

An Introduction to Lenten Praying

The three traditional pillars of Lent are prayer, fasting, and almsgiving. In this book, we honor these pillars through praying, simplifying, and giving. First, praying. What is prayer? How and why do we pray? How can we practice praying individually and as a family? This chapter will guide you through different forms of prayer.

There's no better way to deepen your understanding of prayer than to do it! Over the years I've come to understand how uniquely individual prayer practice can be. There is no "right way" to pray. One prayer practice may resonate with you or someone in your family much better than another. Find which makes your soul sing by experimenting and trying different ways. I believe this is also true for children, so encourage your family members and congregations to approach prayer with a sense of openness and exploration. Over time, and with practice, you'll find the prayer practice that works best for you. Or maybe it's the other way around: The prayer practice that works best for you will find you. Try it and see! At the end of this chapter there is a short exercise to help you talk about the different types of prayer and which type each person found to be the most meaningful.

"Now bow your heads and close your eyes and let us pray" is a phrase I often hear in churches and homes when ministry leaders and parents teach children to pray. I certainly heard it often in my church growing up. As a child, I got the impression that prayer was when we close our eyes and bow our heads and talk to God. There was never any listening involved, and there was never any other way to pray. Even though I have always liked words and talking, it was hard for me to connect to this way of praying as a child and young adult. Even now, as a pastor, I appreciate having other ways to pray. Read on for some ideas you might try with your family members.

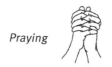

Make and Use Prayer Beads

There are many different forms and styles of prayer beads, used throughout different cultures and religions. You can try this for yourself by making your own. Experiment with what works best. Here are some ideas to try:

- **Four types of prayers.** Pick four different colors to represent different kinds of prayers. One color for gratitude, a second for self, a third for others, and a fourth for the nation and world. Pick a number between two and ten and put that number of beads on your string in each color. (For example: four pink beads to represent gratitude, four green to represent self, four purple to represent others, and four yellow to represent the nation and the world.) The colors and numbers can be arbitrary or have a meaning you assign them. Put a larger bead between each of the sections to divide them.

- **Something to hold.** Prayer beads don't require an organized structure with meaning. They can simply be a collection of beads (with or without a charm) to hold on to while you pray. Get a variety of pony beads and string and make your own string of beads to hold while you say a prayer.

- **Guided and structured.** Investigate different prayer beads and guides and find one that speaks to you or your tradition. Buy or make beads that are appropriate to your family's church history or values.

- **Imagine your own.** Find beads of different sizes, colors, and textures, and create your own beaded prayer journey. One example:

— Start with a big and interesting bead to represent a prayer inviting God to be with you in your prayer time.
— Add three small flat beads to represent prayers of gratitude.
— Add one medium-sized bead to represent silent listening.
— Add two small round beads to represent praying for others.
— Finish with a second large and interesting bead to represent your closing *Amen.*

However you choose to organize your beads, when it is time to pray, practice touching each of the beads as you say your prayer or listen in silence. Adding this physical component to your prayer can help keep you grounded and focused on the present as you pray.

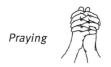

Candle Prayers

Lighting candles to represent prayers is a tradition that spans many centuries, countries, and religious traditions. Candle flames are a simple way to make the prayers of our hearts visible. Here are five different ways to use candles in prayer during Lent. (Choose wax or battery-operated candles depending on the ages represented in your household, and remember never to leave wax candles unattended!)

- **God's love candle prayer.** As you light a candle, say, "The light of this candle represents God's love for us and for all people. Whenever we pass by, we will remember God's love for all." When it's time to blow out the candle, say, "Thank you for your love, God. Amen."

- **Prayers under the candle.** Write the names of the people you would like to lift up in prayer on a piece of paper and place it under the candle. You could also draw a picture of the prayer. As the light of the candle shines, remember the prayer on the paper.

- **Send a candle prayer.** Light a candle and take a picture. Send it to someone you are praying for with a message: "This candle is a prayer for you. Thinking of you and sending you love."

- **Specific prayer.** When you have something specific to pray for, say the prayer out loud and then light the candle. "God, this candle is my prayer for _____." When you extinguish the candle, say, "Hear my prayer. Amen."

- **Recognizing the Spirit's presence.** Light a candle before a meal, while having a family conversation, or any time you'd like to mark holy space. Say, "We light this candle as a reminder that the Spirit is present with us." At the end of the holy time, extinguish the candle and say, "Thank you, God, for this holy time. Amen."

Easter Egg Prayers

Fill an Easter basket with open (unassembled) plastic eggs. Encourage family members to write or draw their prayers on slips of paper and close them up in an egg. When all the prayers are hidden inside the eggs and the basket is full, take time to sit together, open the eggs, and read the prayers. Filling the eggs with prayers can take days or weeks; you might rotate through this practice several times during Lent, or save up all of the prayers until Easter morning and read them together.

Pretzel Prayers

Pretzels have been associated with Lent and Easter for centuries. There's a legend that pretzels were used by an Italian monk to encourage young people to pray. According to the legend, the traditional shape of the pretzel represents arms folded across the body, with hands touching the shoulders—a prayer posture of the time. Pretzels were also popular during Lent because of their sparse ingredient list. People ate simply during Lent, or cut out meat and animal products, and pretzels were made from basic ingredients such as flour, salt, and water.

Try one of these ideas for incorporating pretzels into your Lenten traditions at home.

- If you're a baker (or want to be!), try making pretzels. As you fold them into the traditional shape, cross your arms and put your hands on your opposite shoulders to try out the pretzel prayer posture.
- Have a special pretzel snack time. Before you start, say a simple prayer: "God, we thank you for this snack and for the way the shape helps us remember to pray."
- Research the history of the pretzel in the church and around the world.
- Put one small pretzel on each plate every day from Ash Wednesday through Easter as a special cue to pray.

Body Prayers

One easy way to try something new in your prayer practice is to use your body in prayer. Focusing quietly with folded hands and a bowed head is surely one way to pray, but there are many other postures and ways to orient your body in prayer. Try one of these.

- **Kneeling.** Try kneeling with hands folded, or kneeling with your body folded over your knees.
- **Lying flat on your back.** Try this one outside on a beautiful day, or at night under the stars.
- **Lifting hands high.** Try offering prayers of gratitude from this position.
- **Sitting.** Pray with hands gently in your lap, or holding hands around a table.
- **Walking.** Sometimes the walk can be a prayer all on its own.
- **Wiggling.** The preferred prayer position of many a young person! If your body wants to move, sometimes letting it move is the best course of action.
- **Adding motions to a prayer.** Make up your own motions to a familiar prayer, such as the Lord's Prayer.
- **Dancing.** Dance freely to music or silence, or try out classical dance positions as you pray.

As you test out the different prayer positions, ask yourself or other members of your family "How did that position feel during prayer?" or "How did I feel connected to God in this prayer position?" Over time you might discover that one position or another becomes a favorite.

Labyrinth Prayers

The labyrinth is an ancient prayer practice where one prays by walking. There are many labyrinth styles, but they are different from mazes—there is always one way in and one way out. Walking a labyrinth is a unique experience. For some people, the first experience of walking a labyrinth is meaningful and transformative. For others, it is a practice that takes time to develop. There are many public labyrinths, and taking the time to find and walk one is a worthy investment of time and energy. Apart from walking a labyrinth, you can experiment with making a simple finger labyrinth. Instructions are available in my first book, *Faithful Families: Creating Sacred Moments at Home,* or through an internet search. Simple prayer labyrinths for walking can also be created in your yard or church parking lot with chalk, string lights, or a projected image. Go on a labyrinth prayer journey during Lent and be transformed.

Jelly Bean Prayer

There are a few versions of the "jelly bean prayer" floating around. Many of them focus on the sadness of Jesus' execution and death; I wrote the following alternative, centered around the new life of the resurrection. Gather jelly beans in the following colors: red, black, green, white, pink, yellow, and orange. As you say the prayer, line up the jelly beans and look at them. When you're done, eat the jelly beans!

> **Red** is the robin; we see her in spring.
>
> She feeds her babies, sheltered under her wing.
>
> **Black** is the soil where seeds sprout and grow.
>
> Look closely and see so much life down below.
>
> **Green** are the leaves on the flowers and trees.
>
> They shelter the animals, insects, and bees.
>
> **White** is the color of the clouds way up high.
>
> What interesting shapes do you see in the sky?
>
> **Pink, yellow,** and **orange** make a beautiful sunrise.
>
> It reminds us of hope. It's a daily surprise.
>
> All of these colors are the colors of spring
>
> They show us God's love and the new life God can bring.

The Daily Examen

The Daily Examen is an ancient way to reflect on your day. To practice it, answer four questions. When practicing the Examen in a group, you can go through the questions one at a time, or you can have each person answer all four questions before moving on to the next person.

1. **Was there something memorable that happened to you today?** Or, If you could remember one moment from today by taking a picture in your mind, what would it be? Describe the picture in your mind with as much detail as you can.

2. **Was there a time when you felt close to God (or the Spirit) today?** If nothing comes immediately to mind, consider these questions: Did you see something beautiful today? Was someone particularly kind to you today? Did your heart feel at peace today?

3. **Was there a time when you felt far from God (or the Spirit) today?** If nothing comes immediately to mind, consider these questions: Was there a time when you felt sad or lonely today? Did you witness anyone acting in a way that was unkind? Did you feel anxious or unsettled today?

4. **What from today are you grateful for?** Think of reasons to be grateful, from the deep and profound (life itself) to the ordinary things you might ordinarily pass by (such as the smell of cinnamon rolls).

End the exercise with a few seconds of silence and by saying, "Amen."

Flower Prayer

Scatter a number of cut flowers (from your garden or the store) around your family table. Place a vase in the center with water. As you sit around the table, have everyone take turns saying a joy, a gratitude, or a concern while placing a flower into the vase. After the prayer is completed, admire your pretty vase of flowers and all the prayers that accompanied them.

How Do I Connect to God in Prayer?

There is more than one way to pray to God. This chapter has a variety of different ideas and options. After you've tried a few, talk about it as a family. Which did you like best? Which helped you talk to God or hear from God? Which would you like to try again? Which did you like the least? Compare your answers to the answers of your friends and family. You might discover that everyone likes to talk to God in different ways!

Chapter 4: Simplifying

Simplifying vs. Fasting

The second pillar of Lent is fasting. Traditionally, Christian fasting has meant abstaining from food, either on a particular day of the week, or for the whole season of Lent. Over time, Christians have expanded on the idea of fasting from food and taken to fasting in other ways, such as giving up sugar or screens. The practices in this chapter take the tradition of fasting in a slightly different direction by encouraging families to simplify in various ways. Instead of focusing on what is being given up or taken away, the focus of these practices is on what is added or appreciated. I find this approach works well with children and eases them into the practice of fasting, which they can explore differently later in life. I encourage you to choose one of these ways to simplify, be it for a small portion of Lent or the whole season.

Head Outside

Instead of: Giving up screens or reducing screen time

Try: Heading outside

Screens are part of our life now, in just about every imaginable way. From navigating directions to taking photos to playing games, I know I'm not alone when I say I have a cell phone near me at (almost) all times. The same is true for our children. Many people lament the use of screens or feel guilty about their screen time and screen usage. Instead of becoming overwhelmed with guilt or spinning your wheels figuring out what to do, try tracking the amount of time you spend outside instead. Make a habit of keeping the screens inside (or turn them on Do Not Disturb mode) while you're outside so that *by default* being outside means no screens. You'll add the beauty and wonder of the outdoors into your life and perhaps discover that the riches you find there bring peace of mind, joy, and excitement. There are so many things to do outside; you can find ideas in this book and elsewhere. The outdoors is full of unexplored treasures!

Lenten challenge for heading outside: How many hours can you log outside this Lent?

Drink Water

Instead of: Giving up sugary drinks

Try: Drinking water

Clean water is truly a miracle and a luxury much of the world does not enjoy. We who can access clean water from our taps may be tempted to take it for granted. It's not that we mean to be ungrateful, but clean water is such a part of our daily lives that we tend to pass by the miracle. In our family, we're used to "special drinks" with dinner (usually sparkling water mixed with juice). Sometimes we neglect the opportunity to drink cool, clean water and enjoy it. Drinking water with meals for a season brings this focus to mind. As you drink water, deliberately thank God for it.

Lenten challenge for drinking water: How many days can you drink water with your meals instead of something different?

Enjoy More Fruits and Vegetables

Instead of: Giving up meat

Try: Enjoying more fruits and vegetables

Ecologists and climatologists tell us that the amount of meat we consume has a tremendous negative effect on the planet. There's great value in consuming less meat and going vegetarian, even for one meal per week. But instead of focusing on giving up meat, turn your focus to enjoying vegetables and fruits. Diets are unique to each family and culture, so I hesitate to speak specifically about what foods to eat and how (clergy and ministry leaders, we would do well to remember this), but a simple challenge to enjoy a bounty of fruits and vegetables is one way to gradually decrease our consumption of meat.

Lenten challenge for enjoying fruits and vegetables: How many different preparations or types of fruits and vegetables can you try this Lent?

Make Something You Would Normally Buy

Instead of: Giving up shopping or spending

Try: Making something you would normally buy

Our culture is definitely a "buy it, use it, throw it away" type of culture. The ability to buy what we need, on demand, without much thought has pros and cons. One con is the amount of waste created when we buy something we don't really need, or the way buying something ready-made can stifle creativity. Instead of buying a new basket, is there a box lying around you might beautify instead? Instead of buying the latest toy, can you use your imagination and make one?

Lenten challenge for making something you'd normally buy: Can you make five things you'd normally buy this Lent?

Compliment Others

Instead of: Giving up negative talk

Try: Focusing on complimenting others

Have you ever noticed how nice it feels when someone says something nice about you? What a lovely and wonderful way to help someone feel special. It takes very little time to compliment someone else, and it gets easier with practice. Sometimes it's easy for us to compliment someone's looks or what they're wearing. Try to compliment the deeper attributes about them, too, such as their creativity when they've made something, or the thoughtfulness of their ideas, or the way they make you feel comfortable when you're around them.

Lenten challenge for focusing on complimenting others: Can you compliment three people per day during Lent?

Enjoy More Books

Instead of: Giving up internet scrolling or games

Try: Reading books or listening to audiobooks

So many people want to add more reading into their everyday life. Even those who don't have this goal seem to feel happier and more fulfilled when they start reading more. We might think we don't have time to read, but when we add up the time spent on video games or internet scrolling, there's a significant amount of time that might be better spent reading or enjoying a full book. Try keeping a tally of the books or audiobooks you enjoy each week. Enjoy them individually and discuss them with the family, or read the same book together as a family. Even ten minutes here and there will add up to something significant over time.

Lenten challenge for reading more books: How many books can you read this Lent?

A Prayer for Simplifying

God, when many things compete for my attention, help me to focus on one thing at a time. When things are messy in my space or in my mind, help me to be gentle with myself as I sift through and keep only what is needed. Amen.

A Prayer for Letting Go

God, there are some things I'd like to leave behind and let go. Help me to gently leave them in the past as I look toward a healthy future where I am kind to myself, others, and the world.

A Prayer for Saying Thanks

Thank you, God, for the gifts of sunshine, air, and water. Thank you for the gifts of smiles and words and each other. Help us to recognize these free and simple gifts you freely give us, all around us, each and every day. Amen.

Chapter 5: Giving

An Introduction to Lenten Giving

The third pillar of Lent is almsgiving. I've shortened this to the simple word *giving,* though I encourage you to use whichever term is most comfortable for you and your family. To give alms is to give money or food to the poor. Giving alms (or charity) is a hallmark of all the world's major religions, something most religious people consider essential. Personally, when I feel like my faith is faltering or fragile, giving to others breathes new life. A giving practice deepens and enriches our faith.

As you set out on your Lenten journey of giving, here are a few general guidelines for consideration.

- **We are all receivers, just as we are all givers.** White people (like me) need to be especially sensitive to this, otherwise we may reinforce stereotypes that *we* (white people) help *them* (people of color). This is a dangerous way to view the world and can lead to paternalism and white-saviorism. As we give to others, we should seek to give with humility, recognizing that all people have gifts to give to others, and that we ourselves need others' care.

- **Charity without justice can perpetuate inequality.** Many of the practices in this chapter are simple gestures that don't address the deeper problems in our society. For example, giving food to a food pantry without working to change the policies keeping people from being able to afford their own food is a partial solution. In many cases, merely offering charity can make problems worse. Children are never too young to learn about justice and inequality.

- **We are always learning and growing as we give and receive.** I recently read an article that fiercely debated whether or not it was good to give bread to ducks. Some argued that bread could harm the ducks much more than it helped, as vital nutrients were missing if a duck's belly overflowed with bread. Others pointed out that when the ducks in a certain area were not fed the bread they had previously been given, they died. This article highlights the danger of two extremes. On one extreme, we give carelessly without asking the question, "Is this what the person needs?" or "Is there a way I could work toward justice in order that all might have what they need?" On the other extreme, we do nothing at all, waiting for a better or perfect solution. For example, I used to hold on to my money when I passed someone on the street

looking for a handout, because I was taught it could do more harm than good. Siblings from other religions taught me that their faith calls them to give without reservation. That teaching sat well with my spirit. I no longer hold back on giving a dollar or two to the person on the street who is holding out their hat for help. I *also* give to organizations that work toward systemic change. This is a worthy balance, I think. Most importantly, as we learn new information and grow and change, we change how we give. We are constantly learning and improving, but we should not wait until we have gained all wisdom to follow our conscience.

Gifting a Box of Favorite Things

In previous books, I've encouraged families to set out a box for a period of time, adding a food item or personal care item each day to the box. At the end of the period, give the box of goods to a local food pantry or shelter that could use them. This practice, a "favorite things box" is similar, but with a twist inspired by my friend Amelia Richardson Dress and her book *The Hopeful Family*.[1]

Instead of placing random items in the box, make a deliberate effort to fill the box with each person's favorite things. Not just any breakfast cereal, but the beloved extra amazing breakfast cereal you only get on special occasions. Not the most inexpensive shampoo you find on discount, but your beloved luxury shampoo that you would give to your best friend as a treat. Giving by sharing the absolute best of what we have to offer does a few things. First, it reminds us that those who are in need of charity deserve more than just the leftovers or the castoffs. Second, it reminds us to treat others with high honor, just as we want to be treated. Finally, it creates a feeling of true joy and excitement around giving. Everyone in your family will love to share with one another what they've chosen to give, and why.

---

1 Amelia Richardson Dress, *The Hopeful Family: Raising Resilient Children in Uncertain Times* (New York: Morehouse, 2021).

When it comes to selecting where to give your box of favorite things, consider giving to a pantry or shelter that offers clients the opportunity to choose which items they receive. In that way, your favorite things might be selected by someone who is looking for just that item. Give your best, as often as you can, and make it a habit.

Giving to Neighbors: Paper Cone Baskets

The greatest commandment in the Bible is to love God with all our heart, soul, mind, and strength, and to love our neighbors as ourselves. One way to love our neighbors is to share joy and delight. This practice is simple and fun, and a great way to share joy and delight with neighbors, whether you live in an apartment or a house.

Make a paper basket by rolling a piece of sturdy paper into a cone shape. Tape or glue the cone shut. Add a handle made from twine or string. (If you're having trouble visualizing this, search "paper cone basket" for an internet tutorial.) Fill the basket with flowers, baked goods, or other treats for your neighbors and add a small note saying, "With love, from your neighbors." You can sign your note or leave it anonymous—whichever you like. Enjoy the feeling of making your neighbors smile.

Giving to Nature

If we think of the world as God's precious creation to be treasured and shared, we will be motivated to care for and protect it. There are many simple ways to care for the earth as a spiritual practice. Try one practice throughout the season of Lent, or pick several to try as the weeks go by.

- Pick up trash around your home, favorite park, church building, or community. Recycle what can be recycled.
- Start a vegetable garden.
- Research native plants and plant them in your home or faith community's garden.
- Reduce the amount of trash your family produces by using reusable containers and water bottles.
- Research ways to reduce your family's water consumption.
- Take cloth bags to the grocery store.
- Change the lightbulbs in your house to more energy-efficient models.

In addition to doing these practices yourself, try to inspire your church community or neighbors to do them together and increase their impact.

Writing Letters for Justice

One of the most powerful gifts we can give another is freedom from an unjust system that is oppressing them. Sometimes we may feel as if there's nothing we can do to impact large and powerful systems, but there are many people and organizations who can help us work for change. Writing letters or postcards is a practice and action that even the youngest among us can participate in. Two organizations that offer great toolkits and resources for letter writing are Bread for the World (look for their "Offering of Letters" campaign) and Amnesty International (look for their "Write for Rights" campaign).

After you write your letters, say a prayer or blessing over them using the prayers in this chapter or your own words.

The Gift of Receiving: Learning to Accept Gifts from Others

As I mentioned at the beginning of this chapter, it is important to receive as well as to give, both to remind ourselves that we are all givers and all receivers, and to stay away from patterns of toxic charity. When we open ourselves up to receive from others, we practice humility. We also give others a gift. When you give to others, how do you feel? Great, right? When you allow others to help you, you are giving them the gift of being a helper. Here are some ways to practice being a good receiver of gifts and charity.

- If you find yourself in need of food, money, or other assistance, know and believe that there is no reason for shame. You can communicate this to your children as well by saying, "Sometimes we have needs and can accept help. Other times we can help others. Right now, we need extra food, so it's our turn to accept help. There are other ways that we can help others now, and some day, it will be our turn to share our food or money."

- If you are serving others in a food pantry, shelter, or other setting, step out from behind the role of "server" and have a conversation with the clients. Sit together at the same table and share the gift of conversation.

- If you are sick or in need, and a friend makes a specific offer of help such as "I'd like to bring you dinner" or "Can I clean your house?" respond with "That is so generous and kind of you. I would love that" instead of "Oh no, I couldn't" or "No, I'm fine." Know that you are giving the giver a gift, and you are modeling to yourself and others the importance of being a receiver. If we aren't able to receive, we shouldn't be giving. Insisting on always being the giver is a form of pride and arrogance.

Giving a Gift to Yourself

I recently heard a story about an adult who was struggling with feelings of worthlessness. He had been taught the acronym JOY, which stands for "Jesus-Others-You." He said it was explained to him that he should always put himself last; because of this, he didn't acquire the skill of checking in with his own needs as an adult. There is plenty of biblical support for caring for others, and an attitude of humility is certainly important. Still, that story inspired me to include a practice in this chapter on giving to yourself. When our faith teaches us to ignore our own needs regularly, nobody is served. Like the often-quoted reminder to put on our own oxygen masks first before assisting others, it's good to make self-care an important part of your spiritual routine. Parents and caregivers can model this for children and one another by speaking openly about the steps they take. "I'm taking some time to chat with someone about my problems because I know I need to take care of my health," or "I've asked my friends to pray for me, because I could use some spiritual support."

The idea of giving a non-tangible gift to yourself might be a little abstract for very young children, but those who are older (the teens and adults in your family) can go around the circle and talk about what gift you want to give to yourself in the upcoming week. It could be a walk, a nap, a conversation with a friend, or something different. Talk with your family members about how you can support one another as you give yourself a gift.

A Prayer Celebrating Uniqueness

In our world there are...

many sizes

many ages

many colors

many shapes

many languages

many ideas

many perspectives

many moods

many personalities.

May we see the image of God in one another. Amen.

A Prayer about Love and Neighbors

When we love our neighbors, we love God.

When we love God, we love our neighbors.

Loving God and loving our neighbors is the center of our faith.

Amen.

A Prayer for Justice

God, we know that all people are made in your image,
but not all people are treated fairly on earth.
Help us to understand how others feel and how to work
for justice
even when it's hard,
even if we need to apologize,
even if hurting others wasn't on purpose,
even if we need to try again and again.
May we know when it's time to listen
and when it's time to speak.
Amen.

A Prayer for Compassion

God, may we always seek to understand other people by listening, by observing, and by learning. Help us to care for other people deep within our hearts and know that God loves everyone, even people we don't like or understand. Even if we need to stay away from someone who is mean or unsafe, may we always remember that everyone is loved, loved, loved. Amen.

Chapter 6: Symbols

Introduction to Symbols

Many years ago, I used Resurrection Eggs as a teaching tool for the story of Christ's death and resurrection. If you're not familiar with them, resurrection eggs tell the story of Christ's death and resurrection by using twelve small symbols, each hidden inside a plastic Easter egg. One at a time each egg is opened, the symbol taken out, and part of the story is told. The symbols vary depending on which version of resurrection eggs one uses, but most feature items such as a tiny crown of thorns representing the one placed on Jesus' head to mock and humiliate him, nails to remember Christ's being nailed to the cross, a spear to remember how Jesus was pierced in the side, and a small sponge representing the one given to relieve Jesus' thirst while he hung on the cross, dying. The symbols are miniature and fit inside the eggs. The minds these eggs are intended to teach are also small, impressionable, and vulnerable. Over the years I've thought about resurrection eggs and wondered, *Are these the symbols that most clearly show our children the meaning of Christ's life, death, and resurrection for our faith?* No one could argue that the symbols used in the resurrection eggs aren't biblical. The crown of thorns, nails, sponge, and spear are all in the story—but are these details of Jesus' death so essential that they must be taught year after year and lifted up over and against other symbols of Jesus' life, death, and ministry?

For me, the answer is a resounding *no.* I love the idea of using plastic eggs with a symbol inside each one to tell the story of Jesus. This is a perfect example of using the cultural tools of the season (plastic Easter eggs) to teach our faith. What I don't like about them is the unnecessary focus on symbols of torture and execution. I'm not arguing that we should shy away from clearly stating that Jesus died. Nor should we shy away from telling truths about state-sanctioned execution in age-appropriate ways. Please don't misunderstand: I am *not* saying we should edit out the hard parts because they are hard. Children are very capable of understanding and grappling with hard and painful realities and, sadly, many are forced to— particularly children who live with daily violence because of systemic injustice. My reason for wanting to edit the resurrection eggs stems not from a desire to censor the truth, but from a desire to lift up the symbols that are essential to the story. The torture and execution of Jesus is not something to be romanticized, glorified, or reduced to child's play. Tiny symbols of torture have no place in plastic eggs.

Christianity has rich symbology that extends beyond the symbols of torture and death. We can tell the story of the life, death, and resurrection of Jesus using a more holistic group of symbols, also drawn from the Bible. In this chapter, I've offered twelve symbols, each from the Bible, that represent Christ's life, death, and resurrection. Four symbols represent Jesus' life, four represent his death, and four represent his resurrection. You are free to use them to create your own set of resurrection eggs, use these short reflections individually to reflect on specific parts of Jesus' story. However you use these symbols, I hope they open your eyes to the possibilities for reimagining which symbols we lift up as we teach our children about Jesus.

Symbols

Life

- Water
- Bread
- Towel
- Fish

Death

- Candle
- Spices
- Linen cloth
- Rock

Resurrection

- Sunrise
- Garden
- Jesus' headcloth
- Empty tomb (leave the egg empty)

Water

Read: Matthew 3:16–17 *And when Jesus had been baptized, just as he came up from the water, suddenly the heavens were opened to him and he saw the Spirit of God descending like a dove and alighting on him. And a voice from heaven said, "This is my Son, the Beloved, with whom I am well pleased."*

Reflect: Water is essential for life! Did you know that the human body is 60 percent water? Our brains and hearts are about 73 percent water, and even our bones are 31 percent water. Without water, human beings cannot survive. We use water every day for drinking, washing, cleaning, and cooking. Water is an important symbol of our faith, too. We are baptized with water, just as Jesus was. Jesus' first miracle was transforming water into wine. Jesus calmed the waters during a storm. Jesus gave several important teachings around water. When we use or drink water, we can remember Jesus' life and teachings.

Practice: Drink a cool glass of water and notice how refreshing it feels. Water gives us life and quenches our thirst. We are made from a lot of water! As you drink your water, say thank you to God for the gift of water.

Bread

Read: John 6:35 *Jesus said to them, "I am the bread of life. Whoever comes to me will never be hungry, and whoever believes in me will never be thirsty."*

Reflect: Do you have a favorite type of bread? Mine is sourdough. I love the crunchy outside and the soft, sour inside. I love to eat my bread with butter or olive oil, or even pesto, which is a green sauce. There are so many different types of bread in the world. Some are hard on the outside and soft on the inside. Some are unleavened, which means they don't rise; they are flat. Some breads have meat or cheese inside. Some are sweet.

Jesus talked about bread and used bread quite a bit in his teaching. In the special prayer he taught us, Jesus said we should ask God for bread every day. He also performed a miracle in which he fed more than five thousand people with just five loaves of bread. Before he died, Jesus said to his friends that eating bread together was one of the ways they could remember him. Bread is so important!

Practice: Bake, eat, or smell bread. As you do, remember how many cultures around the world enjoy bread and eat it every day. And remember Jesus, as he suggested!

Towel

Read: John 13:4–5 *[Jesus] got up from the table, took off his outer robe, and tied a towel around himself. Then he poured water into a basin and began to wash the disciples' feet and to wipe them with the towel that was tied around him.*

Reflect: Have you ever washed somebody's feet? Have you ever had somebody wash your feet? Feet can get dirty from the dust and mud outside. They can get stinky in our shoes and gym socks. Some people have ticklish feet! Jesus washed his friends' feet to care for them and show them love. At first, Peter, one of Jesus' disciples, didn't want Jesus to wash his feet, but later he agreed. Jesus used a towel to dry their feet. When we see a towel, we can remember the love and care Jesus showed to his friends.

Practice: Wash your hands (or someone else's hands) and dry them with a soft and fluffy towel. As you dry their hands, remember what a gift it is to use your hands to serve God and other people.

Fish

Read: Luke 5:4–6 *Jesus said to Simon, "Put out into the deep water and let down your nets for a catch." Simon answered, "Master, we have worked all night long but have caught nothing. Yet if you say so, I will let down the nets." When they had done this, they caught so many fish that their nets were beginning to break.*

Reflect: Some of the earliest followers of Jesus were fishermen. They left their fishing nets to follow Jesus. Fish are a very important symbol throughout the story of Jesus. There are three different miracles involving fish! One involves a miraculous catch of fish. One is a very mysterious story where a money coin is found in a fish's mouth. The third miracle is when Jesus fed five thousand people with bread and fish. There is one more very special way that the fish is a symbol of Jesus. For this, you need to learn a little bit of Greek, the original language of the New Testament. In Greek, the words "Jesus Christ, Son of God, Savior" are: Ἰησοῦς Χρῑστός Θεοῦ Υἱός Σωτήρ. The first letter of each in Greek makes the acronym ΙΧΘΥΣ (IKhThUS), which means *fish*! For this reason, the earliest followers of Jesus used the sign of a fish to represent their faith in Jesus.

Practice: Try to draw the letters ΙΧΘΥΣ in Greek to spell "fish," or color a picture of fish.

Candle

Read: Luke 23:44–46 *It was now about noon, and darkness came over the whole land until three in the afternoon, while the sun's light failed; and the curtain of the temple was torn in two. Then Jesus, crying with a loud voice, said, "Father, into your hands I commend my spirit." Having said this, he breathed his last.*

Reflect: During his life on earth, Jesus performed many miracles, taught many important things, and became friends with many people. When he died, his friends became so sad. In this scripture we hear that the sun's light failed, and the whole earth was in shadow—all the light went away. Sometimes when we are sad after someone has died. It feels like we are in a shadow too. It feels like a cloud has covered our hearts. Former President Roosevelt's wife *and* mother died on the same day. On that day he wrote in his journal, "All the light has gone from my life." I wonder if the disciples felt the same way.

Practice: Light a candle and look at the flame for a few seconds. Read the scripture above and then blow out the candle. After you blow it out, say, "God, even when shadows cover the earth and light is gone, help us to know that your Spirit is with us always. When we miss someone who has died, give us comfort. Amen."

Spices

Read: John 19:39 *Nicodemus, who had at first come to Jesus by night, also came, bringing a mixture of myrrh and aloes, weighing about a hundred pounds.*

Reflect: The gospel story of Mark says that Nicodemus and Joseph prepared Jesus' body for burial with spices and linen cloth. Nicodemus was the one who brought the spices, which were a mixture of myrrh and aloes. He brought a lot of them. So many, in fact, that they weighed one hundred pounds! That's a lot of spices. Myrrh is one of the same spices that the Magi brought to Jesus when he was just a small child. Everyone begins their life as a baby, and everyone eventually dies. Most people live to be old before their death. When we smell myrrh, we can remember that everyone is born and lives and dies. Our spirit comes from God and returns to God, always.

Practice: Put some myrrh oil on a cotton pad and smell it. This is the smell of the spice that was used to prepare Jesus' body for burial. How does it smell to you?

Linen Cloth

Read: John 19:40 *[Nicodemus and Joseph] took the body of Jesus and wrapped it with the spices in linen cloths, according to the burial custom of the Jews.*

Reflect: Nicodemus and Joseph took some time with Jesus' body after he died. Even though it can feel very hard and different, it is a holy gift to be near someone's body after it dies. We might feel scared, but we can remember that death is normal and natural. When an insect or bird dies, we can respect its life by respecting its body. We can carefully bury it or move its body somewhere safe. When Jesus died, Joseph and Nicodemus respected his body and took good care of it. They did so by wrapping it with strips of linen cloth and spices. When they did this, they noticed that his body did not have any more signs of life. He was not breathing. His heart was not beating. His body was cold and pale. He did not look like he did when he was alive. When someone dies, their heart stops beating and their lungs stop taking in new air. Their body is present, but their spirit is gone. When Nicodemus and Joseph spent time with Jesus' body and prepared it with spices, they showed their love for Jesus.

Practice: Hold on to some bands of linen cloth and remember that they were used to show love and respect to Jesus' body after he died. Write the name of someone you love who has died on the cloth and remember them.

Rock

Read: Matthew 27:59–60 *So Joseph took the body and wrapped it in a clean linen cloth and laid it in his own new tomb, which he had hewn in the rock. He then rolled a great stone to the door of the tomb and went away.*

Reflect: In Jesus' time, when people died their body was put inside a tomb. A tomb is like a dark cave. The tomb was a safe resting place for Jesus' body. Joseph gently laid Jesus' body, wrapped in spices and cloth, into the tomb. After that, he rolled a big rock in front of the entrance. The rock was to prevent others from coming in and to keep Jesus' body nice and safe. I wonder if it was hard for Joseph to roll the rock in front of the tomb by himself. Matthew's gospel doesn't say that he had help, but I wonder if he did. The rock was big and heavy. Maybe it was cold.

Practice: Hold a rock in your hand. Is it cold or warm? rough or smooth? As you hold it, think about the large rock that covered Jesus' tomb and remember Jesus and all the miracles he performed in his life.

Sunrise

Read: Mark 16:2 (NLT) *Very early on Sunday morning, just at sunrise, [Mary Magdalene, Mary the mother of James, and Salome] went to the tomb.*

Reflect: Have you ever seen the sun slowly rising in the morning? It can be a magnificent sight! The sunrise happens slowly and majestically, with colors coming into view bit by bit. The darkness eventually fades away until the light of day is everywhere. When the three women went to Jesus' tomb, it started out dark, but bit by bit, the light came. It was a majestic morning. They came expecting to find death but instead found life.

Practice: Watch the sun rise. Take a moment to reflect on the beauty of each stage as the sun gets brighter and brighter. If the weather doesn't allow this, look at pictures.

Garden

Read: John 20:11–18 *But Mary stood weeping outside the tomb. As she wept, she bent over to look into the tomb; and she saw two angels in white, sitting where the body of Jesus had been lying, one at the head and the other at the feet. They said to her, "Woman, why are you weeping?" She said to them, "They have taken away my Lord, and I do not know where they have laid him." When she had said this, she turned around and saw Jesus standing there, but she did not know that it was Jesus. Jesus said to her, "Woman, why are you weeping? Whom are you looking for?" Supposing him to be the gardener, she said to him, "Sir, if you have carried him away, tell me where you have laid him, and I will take him away." Jesus said to her, "Mary!" She turned and said to him in Hebrew, "Rabbouni!" (which means Teacher). Jesus said to her, "Do not hold on to me, because I have not yet ascended to the Father. But go to my brothers and say to them, 'I am ascending to my Father and your Father, to my God and your God.'" Mary Magdalene went and announced to the disciples, "I have seen the Lord"; and she told them that he had said these things to her.*

Reflect: When Mary saw Jesus after he had risen from the dead, she mistook him for a gardener. I wonder why. Many people remind us that the garden is an important symbol in the Bible. The very first humans lived in a garden, the Garden of Eden, where there were all kinds of wonderful vegetation and animals. Jesus talked about seeds growing in different kinds of soil in his ministry. Jesus also cares

for his people with tender care and mercy, like a good gardener.

Practice: Plant some seeds in the earth and remember the resurrection of Jesus in the garden. It will take a while for your seeds to sprout. As you wait for them to grow, remember what it means to wait and hope.

Jesus' Head Cloth

Read: John 20:6–7 *Then Simon Peter came, following him, and went into the tomb. He saw the linen wrappings lying there, and the cloth that had been on Jesus' head, not lying with the linen wrappings but rolled up in a place by itself.*

Reflect: When Peter went into the tomb to find Jesus, he wasn't there. There were, however, some of the cloths that had been wrapped around Jesus' body and one special cloth, the one that had been around his head. That special cloth was rolled up and in a place all by itself. I wonder why. I wonder if there is a special meaning in that headcloth wrapped up and placed to the side. What do you think?

Practice: Find a small dish towel in your home and roll it up. As you do, think about the care and intention that comes from folding or rolling something neatly. Imagine what it might have meant for Jesus to roll up the cloth that had covered his face and put it aside.

Empty Tomb

Read: Luke 24:2–3 *They found the stone rolled away from the tomb, but when they went in, they did not find the body.*

Reflect: When the disciples went to the tomb to look for Jesus, he was not there. The tomb was empty. This is very good news! The disciples didn't understand at first, but then they saw Jesus and talked to him and experienced him. Jesus ate fish with them and shared many more things about God's love. The Bible says that Jesus shared so many wonderful things and did so many miracles that there are not enough books to contain them! Hallelujah! The tomb is empty. Christ is risen! He is risen, indeed.

Practice: Open a plastic egg and notice that it is empty. It is round, like a tomb. Think about the empty tomb, and rejoice in the good news of resurrection! Jesus Christ is risen! Thanks be to God!

Chapter 7: Holy Week

Holy Week

Holy Week is a journey through the most difficult week of Jesus' life, followed by the most joyous day in the Christian year. There are many emotional ups and downs during this week! This chapter takes you through a simple practice and prayer for each day. You'll notice that other chapters in this book put the prayers at the end of the chapter, separating them from the practices. In this chapter, the prayers are interspersed with the practices, and each prayer is listed with its corresponding day. Let these practices be an anchor and a guide to you during Holy Week, but don't feel tied to them. Perhaps your family will want to refer to the practices on just one or two of the days. Perhaps you'll want to do all seven. Blessings to you as you seek God this Holy Week.

Palm Sunday

Read: Matthew 21:1–11 *When they had come near Jerusalem and had reached Bethphage, at the Mount of Olives, Jesus sent two disciples, saying to them, "Go into the village ahead of you, and immediately you will find a donkey tied, and a colt with her; untie them and bring them to me. If anyone says anything to you, just say this, 'The Lord needs them.' And he will send them immediately." This took place to fulfill what had been spoken through the prophet, saying,*

> *"Tell the daughter of Zion,*
> *Look, your king is coming to you,*
> *humble, and mounted on a donkey,*
> *and on a colt, the foal of a donkey."*

The disciples went and did as Jesus had directed them; they brought the donkey and the colt, and put their cloaks on them, and he sat on them. A very large crowd spread their cloaks on the road, and others cut branches from the trees and spread them on the road. The crowds that went ahead of him and that followed were shouting,

> *"Hosanna to the Son of David!*
> *Blessed is the one who comes*
> *in the name of the Lord!*
> *Hosanna in the highest heaven!"*

When he entered Jerusalem, the whole city was in turmoil, asking, "Who is this?" The crowds were saying, "This is the prophet Jesus from Nazareth in Galilee."

Reflect: As Jesus came into Jerusalem, a celebration parade formed. People waved palm branches in the air and laid their coats down like a red carpet for Jesus. Jesus was riding on a peaceful donkey, not a war horse. The way Jesus came through the city was another reminder that following Jesus is a choice to do things differently. The people shouted "Hosanna!" as they waved their branches, which means "Save us!" I wonder what it means to ask Jesus to save us.

Practice: Make a palm branch. An easy way to make a palm branch is by using green construction paper. Draw or trace a design of green palm fronds and attach them to something sturdy such as a pipe cleaner, popsicle stick, or real tree branch. Another way to make the leaves is by tracing and cutting out your own handprints. As you wave your branch, think about how you might celebrate Jesus and everything Jesus taught us while he was here on Earth.

Prayer for Palm Sunday

Today we shout "Hosanna!"

It means "Save us!"

Sometimes we need your help, God.

We turn to you when we need guidance or wisdom.

Help us when we don't know which way to go.

Guide us throughout this Holy Week as we learn and grow in faith. Amen.

Holy Week Monday

Read: Matthew 21:12–13 *Then Jesus entered the temple and drove out all who were selling and buying in the temple, and he overturned the tables of the money changers and the seats of those who sold doves. He said to them, "It is written,*

> *'My house shall be called a house of prayer';*
> *but you are making it a den of robbers."*

Luke 19:41 *As he came near and saw the city, he wept over it.*

Reflect: In these two passages, we see Jesus showing two very different emotions: anger and sadness. Throughout his life, Jesus showed many other emotions, too. Jesus was happy, sad, angry, exhausted, worried, and hopeful. Sometimes Jesus felt even more than one of these emotions on the same day! We are the same. We experience different emotions as we go throughout our days. No emotion is better or worse than another emotion. Each tells us something about what is happening in our body, in our mind, and in our spirit.

Practice: Using a box of crayons or a set of watercolor paints, pick the color that best represents how you're feeling right now. Use it as the primary color in a picture. When you're done, you can share your color and your emotion with someone else, or you can keep it private, just for you.

Prayer for Holy Week Monday

On this day Jesus was angry, sad, and tired.

Sometimes we are angry, sad, and tired too.

God, please be near us no matter how we feel,

and help us remember you are always with us, no matter what. Amen.

Holy Week Tuesday

Read: John 12:35–36a *Jesus said to them, "The light is with you for a little longer. Walk while you have the light, so that the darkness may not overtake you. If you walk in the darkness, you do not know where you are going. While you have the light, believe in the light, so that you may become children of light."*

Reflect: Before Jesus died, he prepared his disciples for the fact that he wasn't going to be around much longer. He reminded them that while the light *was* with them, they should enjoy it and walk with it and believe in it. There is always time for grief, but taking time to enjoy the good things you have while you have them is a very important lesson to learn.

Practice: Light a candle (or turn on a battery-operated candle) and enjoy the light that it shines. Think about some of the blessings you have in life; list them out loud if you'd like. When we take something for granted, it means we don't enjoy it while we have it. Use this practice as a reminder not to take anything for granted in life.

Prayer for Holy Week Tuesday

God, please help us to enjoy the people we love while we have them with us. Help us to remember that each day is a precious gift. Amen.

Holy Week Wednesday

Read: John 12:36b *After Jesus had said this, he departed and hid from them.*

Reflect: Here's something interesting: the Bible is silent about exactly what Jesus did on Wednesday after he went away from his disciples. Why do you think that is? Maybe he needed to rest after a very busy couple of days. Maybe he needed a nap. Maybe he needed reflection. The Bible doesn't say. I wonder what it was Jesus did on that day.

Practice: In honor of the fact that the Bible is silent for a day during Holy Week, take time to practice silence today. Practicing silence is not easy! Sometimes it can be quite hard. At first, try silence for just one minute. While you are silent, you can feel the air going in and out of your nostrils. You can look around at your surroundings. You can listen to the noises around. Try to only listen. Don't talk. Once you've tried silence for one minute, try it again for three minutes. Try for five minutes, or even ten. Do you think you could be silent for thirty minutes or even an hour? Give it a try and see how it goes.

Prayer for Holy Week Wednesday

God, please help us develop a practice of silence. While we try to ignore all the distractions around us and be still, please help our chattering minds return to the silence. May we hear your voice in quiet moments. Amen.

Holy Week Thursday

Read: Mark 14:22–24 *While they were eating, he took a loaf of bread, and after blessing it he broke it, gave it to them, and said, "Take; this is my body." Then he took a cup, and after giving thanks he gave it to them, and all of them drank from it. He said to them, "This is my blood of the covenant, which is poured out for many."*

Reflect: Jesus ate bread and wine with his friends and told them that this was a very special reminder of who he is. Bread is such an important part of the meal. Many different cultures eat bread, and there are many different kinds. I wonder why Jesus said that the bread was his body when he was talking to the disciples. I wonder what that means.

Practice: Bake bread and smell the wonderful smell inside your home. If you don't have time to make an entire recipe, try making bread from a pre-made loaf that only needs to be heated, or baking rolls from a can that you can place on a cookie sheet. Choose a bread that fits your family culture and dietary restrictions and feel free to use an expansive definition of what bread means to you. Let the bread you choose be a symbol of the holy meal Jesus ate with his friends. You can share your bread with your friends and neighbors.

Prayer for Holy Week Thursday

When we smell the wonderful scent of baking bread or eat a freshly baked loaf, may we remember that special meal Jesus had with his disciples. May we remember that, just as Jesus ate around a table with his disciples, he is near to us, too. Amen.

Holy Week Friday

Read: Matthew 27:45–50 *From noon on, darkness came over the whole land until three in the afternoon. And about three o'clock Jesus cried with a loud voice, "Eli, Eli, lema sabachthani?" that is, "My God, my God, why have you forsaken me?" When some of the bystanders heard it, they said, "This man is calling for Elijah." At once one of them ran and got a sponge, filled it with sour wine, put it on a stick, and gave it to him to drink. But the others said, "Wait, let us see whether Elijah will come to save him." Then Jesus cried again with a loud voice and breathed his last.*

Reflect: Jesus took his last breath on the Friday of Holy Week, and then he died. The details of his death are extremely hard and sad. Jesus felt abandoned when he died. It was a tragedy. We might already know how this story ends, but even if we do, it can be good to sit for a minute with the sadness and shadows of this dark day. When someone dies, or when something sad happens in our lives, we don't need to rush ahead to feel better or okay. It's fine (and sometimes even good) to take the time to be sad and remember that sometimes sad things happen in life that we can't stop.

Practice: Light a candle. You might want to light the same candle you lit on Tuesday. Sit with the light for a brief time and then blow it out with a sharp breath. As you sit in the shadows with the light gone away, how do you feel? Write down how it feels to remember the day Jesus died, or draw a picture. This is a hard and sad practice. Consider ending your time with a family hug so everyone leaves the practice feeling safe and secure.

Prayer for Holy Week Friday

The day Jesus died was such a sad day. Darkness covered the whole earth. God, please be near to us when we are sad about the death of Jesus or the death of anyone we love. Draw near to us when we grieve. Amen.

Holy Week Saturday

Read: Matthew 27:66 *So they went with the guard and made the tomb secure by sealing the stone.*

Reflect: On the day before Jesus rose from the dead, guards and soldiers made sure his tomb (the place where they laid his body) was sealed shut. They didn't want anyone to steal his body, and they wanted to make sure nobody could lie about his being raised from the dead. So they sealed the tomb up tight around the stone and put a guard there to watch it.

Practice: Find a rock somewhere outside. Make sure it's a rock you will be able to find again tomorrow. Take note of where it is outside, but don't touch it or move it. While you are looking for it, think about how you will go to this same place tomorrow.

Prayer for Saturday of Holy Week

God, on Holy Saturday we wait and wonder. We wait for Jesus to rise from the dead, just as he said, and we wonder what was happening in that empty tomb. Help us to wait and wonder with hope in our hearts. Amen.

Easter Sunday

Read: Mark 16:2–5 *And very early on the first day of the week, when the sun had risen, they went to the tomb. They had been saying to one another, "Who will roll away the stone for us from the entrance to the tomb?" When they looked up, they saw that the stone, which was very large, had already been rolled back. As they entered the tomb, they saw a young man, dressed in a white robe, sitting on the right side; and they were alarmed.*

Reflect: When the women went to the tomb, they were expecting to find it sealed shut, just as it had been left. But it was open! Jesus had risen from the dead—but they didn't know that right away. They saw the angel, dressed in white, and it scared them at first. Sometimes even good and exciting things can be scary when we're surprised or don't understand what's going on. But this was very, very good news!

Practice: Go and find the rock you looked for yesterday. If it is small enough to bring inside, bring it in. If it is too big to bring inside, see if you can move it, even a little bit, from where it was. As you move your stone, remember the wonderful day when the stone was rolled away from Jesus' tomb and he rose from the dead!

Prayer for Easter Sunday

We started the week by saying "Hosanna!" We end it by saying "Hallelujah!" Thank you, God, for all the good gifts of Easter. Thank you for the hope that comes when the tomb is empty. Christ is risen! He is risen, indeed.

Chapter 8: Easter Vigil and Easter

An Introduction to the Easter Vigil and Easter

The resurrection is one of the deepest mysteries of our faith. Resurrection Sunday is the day when everything changes. Death turns to life. Fear turns to reassurance. Sorrow turns to joy. This chapter provides practices and prayers to help you mark this important day. The Easter Vigil and the Sunrise Breakfast provide practices that ease you into the day, allowing you to take it in slowly. Even if you don't use them every year, I encourage you to give them a try occasionally, for it is important to remember that resurrection sometimes happens slowly, in the dark.[1] As always, the practices in this chapter are meant to be a canvas on which you can paint any of your family's Easter plans and traditions. Christ is risen! Alleluia!

---

1 This idea is thanks to Barbara Brown Taylor, *Learning to Walk in the Dark*.

Light an Easter Vigil Fire

The traditional Easter Vigil is held between the evening darkness of Holy Saturday and the dawn of Easter morning, sometimes just after sunset and sometimes from midnight to three o'clock in the morning. A fire is often lit during the vigil, symbolizing the light of Christ coming out of darkness. Some historians say that the Easter fire predates Christianity and originated as a celebration of the spring chasing away the winter.

You can have your own Easter Vigil fire at home on the Saturday of Holy Week or very early Sunday morning before the sun rises. The fire doesn't need to be fancy or elaborate. Your fire might be in a small outdoor fire pit on a patio, or even a few candles placed together in a group. Traditionally, the Easter Vigil fire is held outside, and the mystery and beauty of the fire creates a sacred space for your family to gather and talk about the good news of resurrection. Here are some things you might do around your Easter fire; choose which one(s) fit your family's style well.

- Read Matthew's account of the resurrection from Matthew 28:1–10. Prompt your family to talk about why the angel might have told the women, "Do not be afraid." I wonder why the angel said that.

- Read Psalm 117 and/or Psalm 118. These Psalms talk about God's faithfulness, and history tells us they were read at the earliest Easter Vigils. Some Easter Vigils still include them.

- Bring out a small white pillar candle to represent the Paschal candle (see the next practice for more on this). Use the light from the Easter Vigil fire to light the Paschal candle, and take it inside your house. When the fire is extinguished outside, the light will remain.

- Research an easy breakfast that can be cooked or warmed over the flames as a celebration of resurrection. Alternatively, bring out a breakfast or midnight snack from your house to eat around the fire.

When you leave your fire or extinguish it, give thanks to God for the gift of life and resurrection by saying, "Thank you, God, for the gift of resurrection and the opportunity to gather around this fire. Amen."

Light a Paschal (Easter) Candle

The Paschal Candle is a white candle lit in the church on Easter and special occasions such as baptisms and funerals. Traditionally, there are four important elements on it:

1. The cross (either a traditional cross or an ornately decorated cross).
2. The Greek letters Alpha and Omega, which signify the beginning and the end. This symbol is taken from the book of Revelation.
3. The year the candle is being used.
4. Five grains of incense that represent Christ's wounds (some people use cloves or brads that can be poked into the candle).

To make a simple Paschal Candle at home, decorate a pillar candle with each of the four elements. One way to do this is by cutting shapes from sheets of beeswax and pressing them onto the candle. Another way is to buy a plain white candle in glass and paint the glass with the first three elements. As I've said, I'm not a proponent of spending time belaboring the wounds of Christ or his torture and suffering. That said, including the traditional incense/cloves on the Paschal Candle is a good way to reference Christ's wounds in a symbolic way. The cloves are a particularly good choice because their scent can bring to mind the spices used to anoint Jesus' body. Try to create small holes in the candle before sticking in the cloves.

You can make a new Paschal Candle every year with a new date on it. Light it on Easter morning, and during the year when someone dies or is baptized. May it be a special candle with a powerful and special meaning: Christ's resurrection is stronger than death.

Sunrise Easter Breakfast

The gospel accounts tell us that the women who went to the tomb on the first day of the week (Sunday) went there very early in the morning. John's Gospel tells us that they went while it was still dark. The truth of the resurrection was revealed slowly as the darkness became light. Have you ever been outside to experience the wonder of a sunrise? Darkness turning to light is a wonderful spiritual experience. The light doesn't come all at once—it comes slowly. Sometimes there are majestic sunrises, where the colors paint up the sky and make you gasp or want to paint a picture. Other times the light comes in on a grey day and you barely notice it unless you are looking for it.

Have breakfast outside on Easter morning, before the sun rises. Notice how the light comes in slowly. Read John 20:1–18, or just eat your breakfast and notice the sun coming into view.

Plant an Easter Garden

When Mary saw the resurrected Jesus in the garden, she thought he was the gardener. Many people say this is *symbolism*. It reminds us of the Garden of Eden God created in the very beginning of the Bible, which was a good and perfect place. There are many ways in which a garden can be a spiritual practice. Every time you look at your garden, you can remember the good news of Jesus' resurrection. Planting a garden, like many things, can be simple or complicated, big or small. I suggest starting with a very small garden, perhaps an herb garden in a pot with two different herbs. As you learn more about plants and gardening, your garden can grow, and you can add to it. Try to remain hopeful and encouraged if your garden struggles or you need to start over. Gardening takes practice and patience.

Host or Contribute to an Easter Meal

After Jesus was raised from the dead, he ate fish on the beach for breakfast with some of his disciples. Eating a meal together was one way to demonstrate that Jesus was raised from the dead in his body as well as his spirit. Plan to have a special meal with your family. Maybe you will want to serve the same food every year. Maybe you will want to have a special drink. (My family loves to have sparkling water with a splash of juice and ice.) Maybe you will want to decorate placemats or napkin rings or put a special candle on the table. If you're attending a meal with someone else, take a moment to think about what you will bring to contribute to the celebration. To eat a meal together with friends and family is a great gift.

The focus needn't be on making something fancy (although sometimes on holidays we like to make things a little special.) The focus for an Easter meal should be on enjoying one another's company and celebrating the good news that Jesus is risen! Alleluia! Whatever you do to celebrate, take time to say thank you to God for the gift of being together.

Share an Easter Gift

The news of resurrection is good news, and it is meant to be shared. It is important to share our faith in ways that are generous and kind and don't impose on other people. The good news of Easter is a gift. It is freely given and freely received. Here are some simple ways to share an Easter gift with a friend or neighbor.

- Give real or crafted flowers.
- Draw a picture of a butterfly or paint a wooden butterfly cutout.
- Make bread or cookies.
- Draw an Easter message on the sidewalk in chalk.
- Make a special card.

With each of your gifts, you might choose to attach a card that says "Happy Easter" or a note that says "For You!" If someone asks you about your faith, be ready to share a story about why Easter is important to you.

Easter Prayers

A Prayer for the Easter Vigil

Before the sun rises on Easter morning, we watch and wait for the day to come. We watch and wait for the good news we know will be here soon. We light a fire and watch the flames light up the night. Thank you, God, for being with us this night and every night.

A Prayer at Sunrise

Night turns to day slowly, slowly.

The shadows fade away slowly, slowly.

God, please help us wait for the sunrise and wait for resurrection slowly, slowly.

A Prayer for Easter Dinner

We sit at the table to celebrate the good news of Easter.

Christ is risen! He is risen, indeed!

We sit together and share a meal.

We also share our stories, and our hope, too.

Christ is risen! He is risen, indeed!

A Prayer for Sharing Easter with Others

Resurrection is a gift to be enjoyed, and also to be shared.

God, help us share the gift of resurrection by loving one another well, caring for one another, and offering gifts of resurrection. Amen!

Chapter 9: The Season of Resurrection

The Season of Resurrection

The church has long agreed that the joyous resurrection is too important to be limited to a single day. There is an entire *season* of resurrection joy to be celebrated! The term for this season is *Eastertide.* I've chosen to go with the simpler "Season of Resurrection" (or simply "Resurrection") to describe this time. To notice resurrection in the everyday is to be in tune with the greatest truth of the Christian faith: death is not ultimately victorious. There is always hope. There is new life all around. This chapter will guide you through ways to practice resurrection all year long. I invite you to let this chapter linger. The official season of Eastertide is 50 days—from Easter until Pentecost. That's a long time to notice (and practice) resurrection!

More Light Every Day—Tracking the Sun

This is one of the only practices in the book that is bound to a geographic location. Friends in the Southern Hemisphere, you can do this practice, but it won't match up with the liturgical seasons of Easter and Resurrection.

In the Northern Hemisphere, the days start getting longer after December 20. Each day brings a bit more light. The change is almost imperceptible, with just a little more sunlight each day. One way to notice this change is to make a sunshine tracker. Each day, mark the time the sun rises and the time it sets. As you do, ask yourself how noticing more and more light makes you feel. I wonder what effect the sunlight has on your mood and well-being.

Rainbows Everywhere

It is amazing to me that one can buy a box of crystal suncatchers for less than ten dollars. So much joy can come from such a little thing! Find or buy a simple crystal suncatcher and hang it in your window where there is often sunlight. Every time you see a rainbow, say a simple word of thanks to God: "Thank you, God, for the miracles of life, light, and color. Amen." This type of spiritual practice is called *using a cue*. The rainbow is your cue to remember. Be delighted by how many rainbows you find in unexpected times and places.

Make a Resurrection Collage

I see resurrection in all kinds of small places all around, especially in the springtime: a baby bird pecking out of her shell, a flower poking out of the earth, rain giving nutrients to the soil. What signs of resurrection do you see all around? Gather up magazines and newspapers (particularly those with lots of photos) and use them to make a resurrection collage. You can add your own illustrations, paintings, or drawings. When you're done with your collage, share it with the other members of your family. Another way to do this is to make one collage as a whole family and work on it together.

Make a Memory Table

When people we love die, they live on in the ways we remember and honor them. The things they taught us and the memories they imprinted on us help us hold on to them. Make a memory table honoring someone you have lost who is important to your family. Gather up pictures of them, along with symbols of their favorite hobbies or music. Put these items together on a table. Add some candles if you like. Once everyone has added to the table, share the memories you have of the person and the things they taught you. Keep their memory alive and vow to honor them with your life. You can close with a simple prayer: "Thank you, God, for all of the ways [NAME] touched our life. Help us to always honor them in the way we live. Amen."

Compost: Turning Waste into Good Soil

One of the greatest examples I know of transformation and resurrection is composting. Food scraps and trash become deep, rich soil. There are many ways of composting, and some require only a small amount of space and minimal effort. Research which method works well for your family and let it be a living experiment of resurrection and new life. If you'd rather not invest in a whole composting system, see if there is a community garden or faith community that composts, and either add your own scraps to it or arrange to visit and learn how it works.

Make Something New Again: Upcycle or Recycle

Another way to make resurrection tangible is to make something old and worn-out new again by recycling or "upcycling" it. Something that may have been discarded for a long time can be given a new life. The internet is full of ideas for this, but here are some very simple ones you might try.

- Turn old and broken crayons into new creations by melting them down in mini muffin tins.
- Make a birdfeeder from a milk jug or paper towel roll.
- Use recyclables such as paper egg cartons and plastic lids to create art.
- Save old glass jars for storage.

Every time you make something old new again, you are practicing resurrection and celebrating life. This practice is also a reminder to take care of the earth God created for us to protect and enjoy.

A Prayer for the Season of Resurrection

When Jesus was raised from the dead, all the people were amazed at what God had done. God, please help us be amazed at the small miracles of resurrection all around us. Sunshine, rainbows, soil, friends, and family all remind us that your presence is everywhere. Thank you for the small and big miracles of life.

A Prayer for Noticing New Life

God, help us to notice and pay attention to the new and growing things all around us:

baby birds in their nests,

buds on plants and trees,

flowers in bloom.

These new things teach us about resurrection and show us the joy of new life.

God, help us to notice and pay attention to the new and growing things all around us.

Chapter 10: Ending the Season

The church year (also called the liturgical year) is organized into seasons, just like the calendar year. Seasons come and go, like waves or circles. We always seem to end up back in the same place, year after year. The rhythm of the seasons can bring comfort at times, and anxiety at other times. When we know a difficult season is coming, we may worry. When an easy season is due to arrive, we anticipate it with wonder and joy. One way to keep an even spirit through the changing seasons is to mark their passing and arriving with rituals and sacred moments. Before jumping into a new season, take time to mark the ending of the old one. The season of Lent is often heavy and full of reflection and introspection. The seasons of Easter and Resurrection can be lighter and full of joy. Before embarking on the season of Pentecost (the next season in the church year), take the time to close the chapter on this overall season of Lent, Easter, and Resurrection. The practices and prayers in this chapter will help you do just that.

Sorting the Symbols of Lent, Easter, and Resurrection

As you look around your home or garden, what symbols seem specific to this season? Perhaps you have an Easter candle on display or other symbols you have used throughout the weeks. Consider what to do with these symbols now as you move into the season of Pentecost. Should they be stored or given away? Is there anything that could be recycled or repurposed into something new? Take a moment to express gratitude for the symbols you have used during this season and find a place for them to live on if they will be useful for the future. If they've served their purpose, don't hesitate to let them go.

Evaluating and Planning for Next Year

As you look back on the season, think about what practices or prayers held special meaning for your family this year. Just because they were useful this year doesn't mean they will be useful next year. That said, take some time to make notes in this book or make a note to yourself for next year. If there's a practice or prayer you feel drawn to, make sure you'll be able to find it easily next year. Put this book somewhere you can find it again for next year's planning.

Planning for Pentecost

The next day and season in the church year is Pentecost. Pentecost is full of great opportunities for family faith formation and personal spiritual growth. The story, found in Acts chapter two, is often called "the birthday of the church." Take a moment to plan how you might celebrate the coming of the Holy Spirit with your family. Some simple ideas include flying a kite or hanging a wind sock (to remember how the Holy Spirit is connected to breath and wind), or baking a cake with your family to celebrate the church's birthday. There are many additional ideas on www.traci-smith.com for you to consider!

A Prayer of Gratitude for the Season

Today we say *Thank you* for the season of Lent.

Thank you for Easter.

Thank you for the season of Resurrection.

In each of these seasons, we have learned something new, and we are grateful.

Thank you, God.

Thank you.

A Prayer for That Which Is to Come

We wait for the next season, the season of the Spirit. Come, Holy Spirit, come. We are waiting for you. Amen.

Acknowledgements

Thank you, first and foremost, to the readers of the other *Faithful Families* books for making them come alive off the page and into real life. The daily work you put into helping the families in your care grow in faith is what motivates me and makes these books successful. I am so thankful for your consistent support and enthusiasm.

Thank you, Brad Lyons, for trusting me, over and over again, and for being there.

Thank you, Catherine McNiel, for endless enthusiasm for my work and for being the floppy hat tulip lady who creates editing magic.

Thank you, Paul Soupiset, for brand magic and all the shades of purple.

Thank you, Jennifer Grant, for waving your fairy wand, time and again, and showing me how it's done.

Thank you, Carol Howard Merritt, for practical hands-on help early on.

Thank you to Daneen Akers, Herb Montgomery, Wendy Claire Barrie, Caryn Rivadeneira, Glenys Nellist, Laura Alary, Arianne Lehn, and Amelia Dress for truly understanding what I'm trying to do with this book and for offering encouraging texts, posts, and for sending positive energy and vibes.

Thank you to Eileen Campbell-Reed and the Writing Table colleagues. Without those morning writing sessions, I would have been truly lost. What a gift you gave me and this book.

Thank you to members and moderators of Speaking of Writing, Forma, Hope4CE, Birthing Cross + Gen Community, and Treasure Box Tuesday. You are the best corners of the internet.

Finally, as always, thank you to my family for being encouraging, supportive, and gracious, particularly my husband, Elias, for unwavering faith in me.